ANIMAL TALK

HOW ANIMALS COMMUNICATE
THROUGH SIGHT, SOUND AND SMELL

WRITTEN BY ETTA KANER

ILLUSTRATED BY GREG DOUGLAS

Kids Can Press

Thank you to Stacey Roderick and Laurie Wark for their patience, attention to detail and thoughtful suggestions; to Greg Douglas for his incredibly realistic artwork and to Marie Bartholomew for her creative design. Thank you also to Dr. Paul J. Watson of the University of New Mexico for his thoroughness and extensive resources for the Sierra dome spider.

To Ora

Kids Can Press acknowledges the financial support of the Government of Canada, through the BPIDP, for our publishing activity.

Published in Canada by
Kids Can Press Ltd.
29 Birch Avenue
Toronto, ON M4V 1E2

Published in the U.S. by
Kids Can Press Ltd.
2250 Military Road
Tonawanda, NY 14150

www.kidscanpress.com

Edited by Stacey Roderick and Laurie Wark
Designed by Marie Bartholomew
Printed and bound in Hong Kong by Book Art Inc., Toronto

The hardcover edition of this book is smyth sewn casebound.

The paperback edition of this book is limp sewn with a drawn-on cover.

CM 02 0 9 8 7 6 5 4 3 2 1
CM PA 02 0 9 8 7 6 5 4 3 2 1

National Library of Canada Cataloguing in Publication Data

Kaner, Etta
    Animal talk : how animals communicate through sight, sound and smell

Includes index.
ISBN 1-55074-982-X (bound).
ISBN 1-55074-984-6 (pbk.)

1. Animal communication — Juvenile literature.
I. Douglas, Greg II. Title.

QL776.K35 2002   j591.59   C2001-901516-X

Kids Can Press is a Nelvana company

Contents

Introduction

How do you tell a friend that you're excited? Do you shout? Do you open your eyes wide? Do you jump up and down? If you do any of these things, you are communicating with your friend. Animals also use their voices and bodies to communicate. Some animals, such as birds, use their voices to attract a mate or to locate each other. A baby penguin can find its mother in a huge crowd of penguins just by listening for her voice. Many mammals use their bodies to greet each other. Elephants touch each other's trunk tips and lions rub their bodies together like house cats.

Besides using their voices and bodies, animals also communicate in more unusual ways. Believe it or not, some animals use flashing lights made with their bodies. Fireflies flash their lights from the underside of their abdomens. Flashlight fish shine theirs from the sides of their faces. Bees communicate by dancing, fiddler crabs by waving, and many animals use smell. No matter how animals send messages, they always seem to understand each other. And you'll get the message, too, when you read about the amazing world of animal communication. To help you understand this world, there are many activities and experiments for you to do. You'll discover how to understand the call of a blackbird, read the body language of a tiger, signal to a firefly and much more.

Emperor penguins

Saying it with sound

Like you, many animals communicate with their voices. Some animals use their voices to warn their group about danger. Males sing to attract females. Mothers call out to find their young. Other animals, such as the howler monkey, loudly announce the borders of their territory. But not all animals make sounds with their voices. Some use tools or unusual parts of their bodies to make noises.

If you were a howler monkey ...

- you would live in the tropical forests of South America.
- you would live in groups of fifteen to twenty males, females and young.
- you would announce your territory by having a group howl every morning and evening. Your group would be heard 5 km (3 mi.) away.
- you would have a bony box in your throat that would amplify your voice, or make your voice louder.

Warning: Enemies are near

"Woof, woof, woof!" shouts a vervet monkey. This means "A leopard is nearby!" As soon as other vervet monkeys hear this warning, they scamper up trees and onto thin branches. They know that a heavy leopard, which can climb trees, could never reach them there. But what if the enemy is an eagle flying above the treetops? Then the signal sounds like "ha-ha-ha." When vervets hear this, they stick close to the tree trunks where an eagle can't fly. A third kind of call — "chut, chut, chut" — warns that a snake is looking for dinner nearby. This call causes vervets to stand up on their hind legs and watch the ground for their enemy.

Vervet monkey

Vervet monkeys aren't the only animals that have different calls for different kinds of danger. The red-winged blackbird has seven alarm calls. The most common one is "check," but it also uses "chuck," "chick," "chonk," "chink," "peet" and "cheer" to warn others about enemies such as raccoons, crows and hawks. When a California ground squirrel sees a hawk, it makes a short, loud warning chirp. But when it sees a snake, it points its tail straight up in the air and wags it quickly back and forth while making a low, staccato sound. The Indian myna bird has three kinds of danger calls: one warns about snakes, the second warns about falcons and the third says that everything is all right once an enemy is gone.

Red-winged blackbird

California ground squirrel

Calling long distance

When an animal wants to claim a territory or advertise for a mate, it often tries to send its message over a long distance. Many animals are able to do this by calling. But some birds don't have loud enough voices to call long distances. They use either hollow or dead wood to help them communicate.

Spotted woodpecker

The spotted woodpecker drums with its beak on a dead branch or a telephone pole. Its beak moves so quickly that its head looks like a blur. What is the woodpecker saying? It might be calling for a mate. Or it might be saying, "This is my territory. Stay away." These messages can be heard 1 km (5/8 mi.) away.

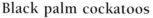

Black palm cockatoos

The huge black palm cockatoo and its mate drum together. Each bird breaks off a small twig with its claws and taps it on a hollow tree. By doing this, the pair is warning others to stay out of their territory.

Knock on wood

Find out why dead or hollow wood carries sound so well over long distances.

You'll need:

a nail

a hammer

a large empty juice can

2 pieces of string, each 30 cm (1 ft.) long

a piece of damp paper towel

1. With an adult's help, use the nail and hammer to make a hole in the middle of the bottom of the can.

2. Tie a knot at one end of one piece of string. Pull the other end of the string through the hole until the knot catches on the inside of the can.

3. Hold the can in one hand. With your other hand, hold the string between the paper towel. Starting at the can, pull the paper towel along the string.

4. Hold the other string in one hand and pull the paper towel along it with your other hand. Which string sounds louder?

When you pulled the paper towel along the first string, the string vibrated, or moved quickly back and forth. The vibrating string shook the air inside the can, which made the string sound louder. This also happens when an animal drums on a hollow log. The log makes the sound so loud that it can be heard far away.

Keeping track

You can likely identify your friends just by their voices. Many animals can do the same. Mothers and babies can find each other in a large noisy crowd by calling out. Mates use their voices to find each other in the dark. And groups of animals use sound to keep track of their members.

After several days of feeding at sea, a mother Steller's sea lion comes back to her rookery, or breeding ground. The rookery has thousands of noisy sea lions in it. When the mother sea lion calls, only her pup, or baby, comes running toward her. Would you do as well in such a large crowd?

Tawny owls hunt for food at night. A pair of owls keeps track of each other in the dark by singing a duet. The first owl sings "to-whit," and the other one immediately answers "oo-oo." These sounds follow each other so closely that people used to think that only one owl was singing "to-whit to-whoo."

Tawny owl

Spiny lobsters make a rasping sound to keep their group together. It sounds like a finger being rubbed along the teeth of a comb. As long as the group hears this sound, it is safe. If a shark or eel shows up for a meal, the sound speeds up and becomes higher. This is the lobsters' warning call.

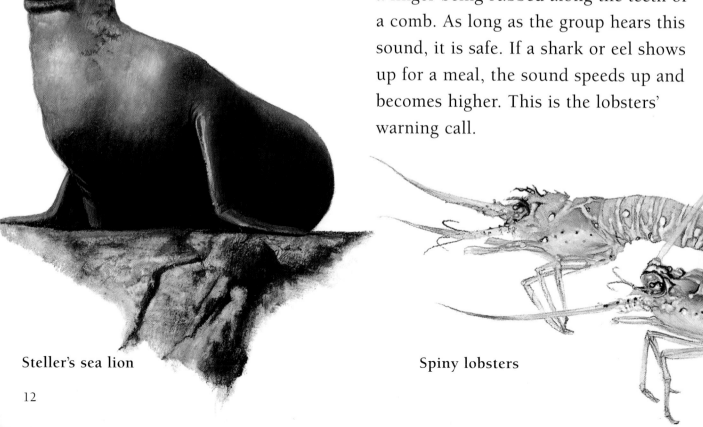

Steller's sea lion

Spiny lobsters

When elephants feed, they try to stay together. But if an elephant is out of sight of the group, the elephant makes a loud purring sound. Other members of the group also purr to let the elephant know that they are nearby. If the purring stops suddenly, it means that an enemy is nearby.

Elephants

Sound you can't hear

Hippos, whales, rhinos and elephants communicate with sound so low that humans can't hear it. This is called infrasound. But even though we can't hear infrasound, we can feel its vibrations in our bodies.

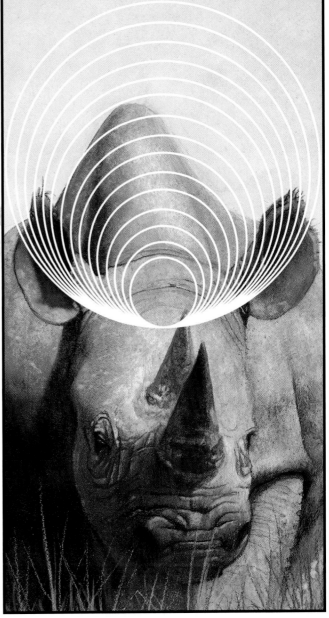

Saying it with smell

Have you ever noticed how often a dog urinates when you take it for a walk? It is leaving a scent, or smell, message that says, "This is my territory." Like a dog, the ring-tailed lemur uses scent to mark its territory. Its scent comes from a chemical made by its body called a pheromone. Many other animals also use pheromones to send messages. Some pheromones tell members of a group where to find food. Others attract mates or warn about danger. Some even help babies find their mothers.

If you were a ring-tailed lemur ...

- you would live on the island of Madagascar, off the southeast coast of Africa.
- you would be about as big as a large house cat.
- you would mark your territory with pheromones that come from glands on your chest and wrists. You would rub the pheromones over your hands, feet and tail.
- you would wave your pheromone-covered tail during a "stink fight" to decide who is the boss of a territory.

No trespassing

Animals try to avoid fighting because they don't want to get hurt. If they are hurt, they will be more easily caught by their enemies. So, to keep away from each other and reduce fighting, animals set up territories. Some mammals mark the borders of their territories with scents. Foxes and wolves leave their scents on rocks, bushes and tree stumps by spraying urine on them. Bison and brown bears urinate on mud and roll in it. Then they rub their bodies against tree trunks, leaving a smelly message for others. Rhinos make a pile of feces and step in it. In this way, they leave their scent wherever they walk.

Some animals use special scent glands on their bodies to mark their territories. They rub their glands on twigs, grasses and leaves. A kind of deer called a klipspringer has a scent gland below its eye. Hyenas have a scent gland between their back legs. When they rub this gland on long grasses, it leaves a white substance that other hyenas can taste and smell.

Klipspringer

Hyena

Waving tails

Find out why ring-tailed lemurs wave their tails at each other during a stink fight.

You'll need:

perfume

a saucer

a blindfolded friend

a piece of
paper towel

1. Pour a few drops of perfume into the saucer and place it about 2 m (6 ft.) from your blindfolded friend.

2. Count the number of seconds it takes your friend to smell the perfume.

3. Take the dish away and wait about ten minutes.

4. Stand 2 m (6 ft.) away from your friend and pour a few drops of perfume on the paper towel. Wave it in the air and count the number of seconds it takes your friend to smell the perfume.

It probably took less time for your friend to smell the perfume the second time. When you waved the paper towel about, you helped the perfume smell move through the air toward your friend. The same thing happens during a stink fight when lemurs wave their smelly tails around.

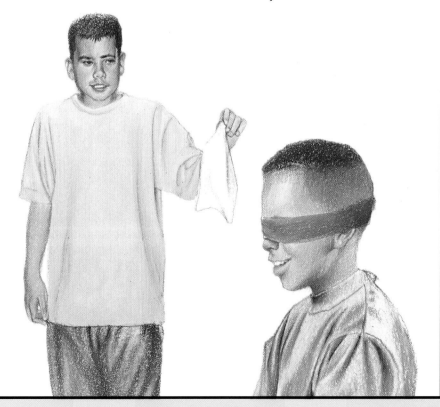

Follow that smell

Do you remember the story of Hansel and Gretel? Hansel dropped breadcrumbs on his way through the forest so that he could find his way back home. Ants do the same thing. But instead of breadcrumbs, they leave a trail of pheromones when they leave their nest. As well as helping an ant find its way home, the trail tells other ants where to find food. Mule deer leave similar messages by rubbing their feet against trees. The scent marks that they leave say to other deer, "This way to good food."

Ant

Some animals follow pheromone trails through the air. When a female silkworm moth wants to attract a male, she gives off a special pheromone called bombykol. As soon as a male senses it, he follows the smell. He might fly as far as 1.6 km (1 mi.) to reach a female. How does the male silkworm pick up a scent so far away? His antennae have fifty million tiny holes that help him "smell" pheromones!

Female silkworm moth

Mule deer

Male Sierra dome spider

What does your nose know?

Can you identify the members of your family by smell? Bighorn sheep can. In fact, that's the only way they know whether another sheep is a relative or not.

If you want to test your nose know-how, put on a blindfold. Then ask your family to sit in a row without talking. Without touching anyone, let your nose figure out who is who.

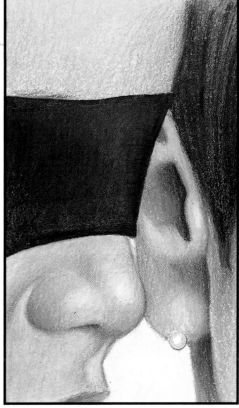

Male Sierra dome spiders are also attracted by a female spider's scent. She covers her web with her "perfume" and waves it in the air. The first male to arrive at the web wants to keep other males away. He rolls up the web into a tight ball so other males aren't able to smell the female's pheromones.

Body language

When animals meet face to face, they often use body language to communicate. The position of their bodies tells animals of the same species, or kind, whether they are relaxed, angry, about to attack or happy to see them. This is especially true of mammals. Mammals can easily move their mouths, eyes, ears and even noses to show how they are feeling. Look at the tiger on this page. What do you think its body language is saying?

If you were a tiger ...

- you would live in Asia.
- you would have a large, white spot on the back of each ear with a ring of black around it. When you were angry, you would rotate your ears to show the white spots.
- you would blink your eyes a lot if you were upset.
- you would flatten your ears against your head when you were about to attack.

About faces

By looking at the positions of its ears, eyes and mouth, you can tell how a mammal feels. Check out these face facts and then test your face-reading skills.

	Position	Message
Ears	ears are facing sideways and slightly forward	I am relaxed.
	ears are pricked up and facing forward	I am alert OR I am listening to something.
	ears are straight out like airplane wings	I won't bother you OR you are in charge.
Eyes	eyes are almost fully open	I am relaxed.
	eyes are half-closed and eyebrows are frowning	I am in danger.
	eyes are closed	I give up.
Mouth	mouth is lightly closed or slightly open	I am relaxed.
	mouth is open with teeth showing	I am angry.
	mouth is open with lips covering teeth	I feel playful.

Read my face

Now that you are an expert face reader, can you tell what these animals are saying?

Chimpanzee

Cheetah

Hippopotamus

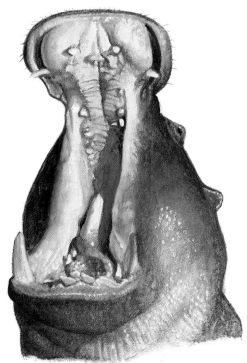

Dog

Answers on page 40

Saying hello

How do you say hello to a friend without using your voice? Do you smile? Do you wave? Do you shake hands? Animals say hello with their bodies, too. Find out how these animals on the African savanna say hello.

Giraffes lick and nuzzle each other's heads, bodies, manes or eyes.

With their ears held high and folded, elephants touch trunk tips. They might even put their trunk tips in each other's mouths.

Male plains zebras sniff each other's noses. Then, with their ears bent forward, they make a chewing motion with their mouths.

Like house cats, lions rub their heads and bodies together.

Sending signals

Imagine that you are a squid. You want to "talk" to another squid, but you can't use sound because squid are deaf. What do you do? You send signals by changing the color of your body. Some birds show their brightly colored feathers to signal others that they've claimed a territory. Others, like this male peacock, use their colors to attract a female. But not all animals send signals through color. Some animals wave parts of their bodies. Others dance. And still others send signals through vibrations.

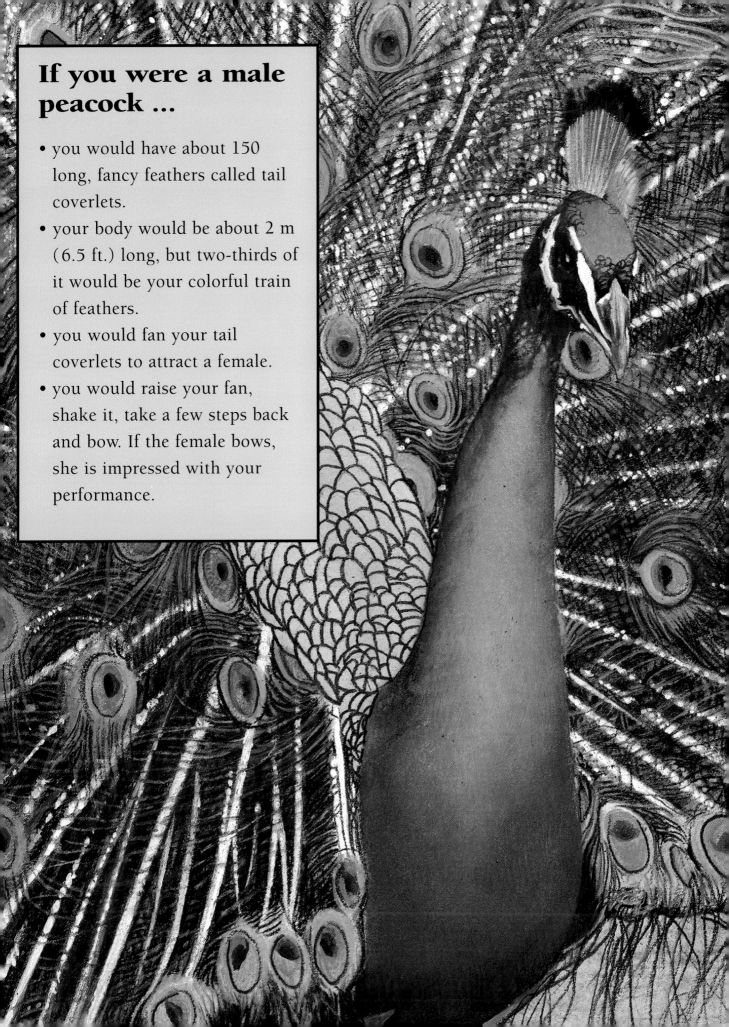

If you were a male peacock ...

- you would have about 150 long, fancy feathers called tail coverlets.
- your body would be about 2 m (6.5 ft.) long, but two-thirds of it would be your colorful train of feathers.
- you would fan your tail coverlets to attract a female.
- you would raise your fan, shake it, take a few steps back and bow. If the female bows, she is impressed with your performance.

Waving animals

Just as you might wave your arm to tell your teacher that you know an answer, some animals wave to send messages. Mudskippers wave their fins at each other to announce their territory. A male fiddler crab waves its giant claw to attract females and to tell other males to stay away. Some male wolf spiders get a female's attention by waving legs with tufts of hair on them. The tufts look like tiny flags that make the spider's signals easier to see.

Now match the waving animals on the right with their messages below.

1. "Get away. This is my mate."

2. "Stop. You are trespassing."

3. "Please come here. I would make a good mate."

Mudskipper

Male fiddler crab

Clawless crabs

People who fish for male fiddler crabs cut off their giant claws for food. Then they throw the crabs back into the sea. This creates a problem for the crabs because without their huge claws, the males can't attract females.

Male wolf spider

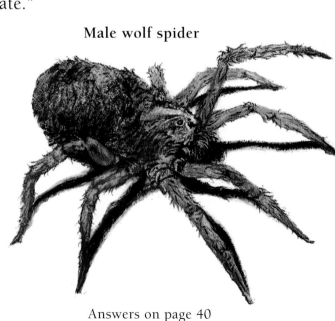

Answers on page 40

Dancing bees

Humans aren't the only ones that dance. Honeybees dance, too. They dance to tell other honeybees that they've found a place with lots of delicious nectar. If the place is close by (less than the length of a football field), a honeybee does a "round dance." If the food supply is farther away, the bee does a "waggle dance." The longer it takes for the bee to do the dance, the farther away the nectar is. How do the other honeybees know in which direction to fly? If the waggle is straight up, the message is "Fly toward the sun." If the waggle is straight down, the message is "Fly away from the sun."

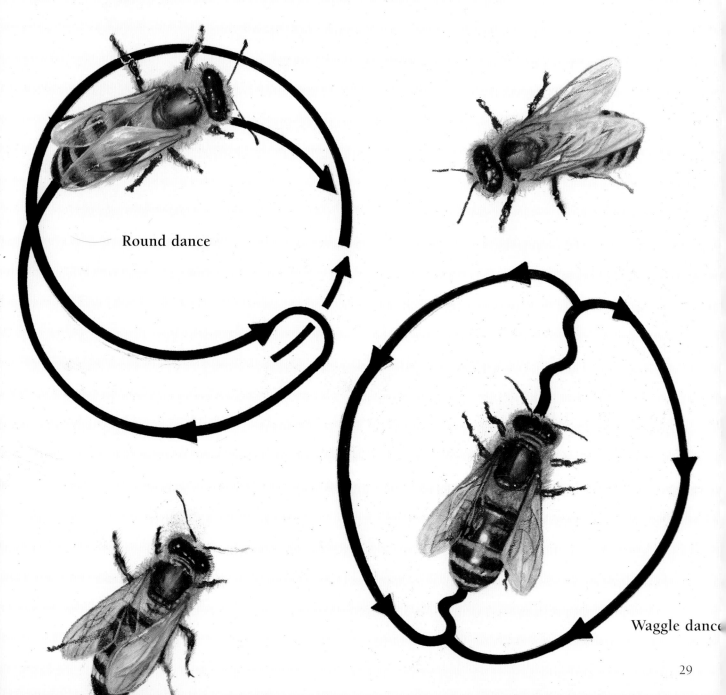

Round dance

Waggle dance

Vibrating signals

Some animals send signals through vibrations. Vibrations happen when something moves rapidly back and forth. If you pluck a guitar string and then touch it lightly, you can feel it vibrate. A hairy mole rat sends vibrations through the earth. As it digs its long tunnel, it frequently hits its head against the roof of the tunnel. It is sending a signal to other hairy mole rats digging nearby. The mole rat wants others to know where it is so that their tunnels won't meet. To receive the vibrating signal, the mole rat presses its jaw against the tunnel wall.

Some male waterstriders use water to send a vibrating message. A waterstrider makes ripples by drumming on the water surface with its midlegs. It might be attracting a female, telling other males to stay away, or trying to protect its territory or food. How do other waterstriders know what the message is? By the speed of the drumming!

A lacewing insect sends its vibrations down a plant stem to another lacewing by shaking its body. Each species of lacewing has its own special rhythm. Its message tells which species it belongs to and therefore whether it would be a good mate.

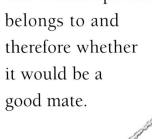

Male waterstrider

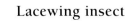

Lacewing insect

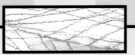

Communicate with vibes

If you want to talk to a friend in a secret code, try using vibrations.
All you need is a long piece of thin string.

1. Tie one end of the string to a table leg and the other end to the knob of a closed door or to the other table leg. Make sure that the string is very taut, or tight.

2. Pluck one end of the string with your fingernail while your friend lightly touches the other end of the string to feel the vibrations. Use Morse code to spell out a secret message, or make up your own code.

International Morse code

A dot is a pluck followed by a very short pause. A dash is a pluck followed by a longer pause.

A . _	H	O _ _ _	V . . . _
B _ . . .	I . .	P . _ _ .	W . _ _
C _ . _ .	J . _ _ _	Q _ _ . _	X _ . . _
D _ . .	K _ . _	R . _ .	Y _ . _ _
E .	L . _ . .	S . . .	Z _ _ . .
F . . _ .	M _ _	T _	
G _ _ .	N _ .	U . . _	

Period . _ . _ . _   Start _ . _   End . _ . _

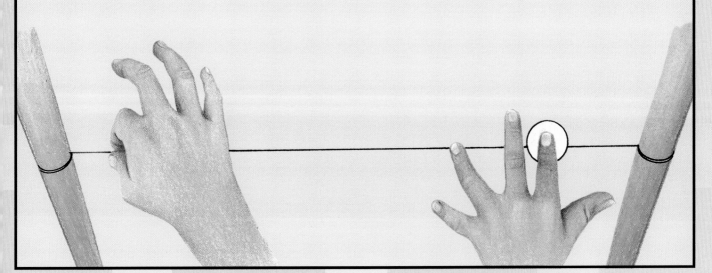

Lighting up

If you dove deep into the sea, at first it
would seem to be totally dark. Then,
suddenly, you would see lights flashing on
and off. The lights would come from the
bodies of fish and other sea creatures. They
would be using their lights to communicate
with each other. If you visited a stream on a
warm summer night, you would see flashing
lights in the air. They would be made by
fireflies signaling to each other. How
do these and other animals send light
messages with their bodies?
Read on to find out.

If you were an adult firefly ...

- you would be a type of beetle with two pairs of wings. You would fly with one pair and use the other pair for balance.
- you would have an organ called a lantern on the underside of your abdomen.
- you would use your lantern to flash a light on and off in a special code to attract a mate. The light would be made by mixing two chemicals in your body with oxygen. This is called bioluminescence.
- you would flash your light at night during mating season in spring or early summer.

Glow in the dark

When a male firefly flashes its light, it's as if he's sending a valentine message to a female firefly. He is saying, "Will you be mine?" Each species of firefly communicates this in a different code. One species might make a series of long flashes every half-second. Another might make two flashes one second apart. The female usually answers with a single flash, saying, "Here I am." How does the male know she belongs to his species? By the length of time she waits before answering.

Many animals that live in the sea also make light with their bodies. Firefleas, which look like tiny shrimp, make green light. They use their light to attract females and to protect themselves. When firefleas turn on their lights, fish are so startled that they drop the firefleas that were about to be their meal.

Flashlight fish also have a greenish light that is made by bacteria, or germs, in pockets on their faces. When flashlight fish greet a friend, they blink their lights on and off very quickly. They do this by opening and closing a cover that works like your eyelids.

Talk to a firefly

If you pretend to be a female firefly, you might get a male firefly to land on your finger. All you need is a tiny flashlight and some patience. Just after sunset in spring or early summer, watch for flashing fireflies. Look for a pattern of flashes, such as three or four flashes in a row. This is a male. Wait for a second or two. Then flash your flashlight for a second. Try this several times. If you are lucky, a male firefly might think you are answering his signal and pay you a visit.

Talking with humans

If animals could talk to us, what would they say? Scientists have been trying to find this out for many years. Since humans don't understand animal talk, scientists decided to teach animals a language that both could understand. This language uses hand signs. Some scientists taught hand signs to dolphins. Other scientists worked with chimpanzees and gorillas. Were the scientists able to communicate with these animals? Read on to find out.

If you were a dolphin ...

- you would communicate with other dolphins by using clicks, grunts and whistles.
- other dolphins would be able to recognize you by your special whistle. This is called your signature whistle.
- your sounds would come out through the blowhole on the top of your head.
- you would also spend a lot of time communicating by rubbing against other dolphins.

Talking with Ake, Washoe and Koko

In an experiment in Hawaii, a trainer taught a dolphin named Ake about forty hand and arm signs. He used these signs to give Ake commands. For example, if the trainer signed "frisbee fetch ball," Ake would take the frisbee to the ball. But if the command was "ball fetch frisbee," Ake would take the ball to the frisbee. This showed scientists that a dolphin can understand word order as well as signed words.

While dolphins do a great job of understanding humans, scientists have a hard time interpreting their clicks, grunts and whistles. Scientists find it easier to understand apes such as chimpanzees and gorillas. That's because

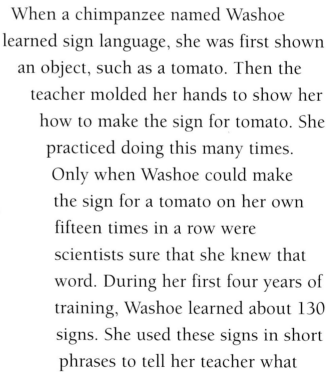

Ake

some apes can "talk" to humans in a language that they can understand. In other words, apes can learn to use sign language.

When a chimpanzee named Washoe learned sign language, she was first shown an object, such as a tomato. Then the teacher molded her hands to show her how to make the sign for tomato. She practiced doing this many times. Only when Washoe could make the sign for a tomato on her own fifteen times in a row were scientists sure that she knew that word. During her first four years of training, Washoe learned about 130 signs. She used these signs in short phrases to tell her teacher what

Washoe

she wanted. She also used them to name things that she had never seen before. The first time Washoe saw a swan, her trainer asked her what it was. Washoe made two signs — one for water and one for bird.

Another ape that learned sign language was Koko, a gorilla. Koko's trainer had to teach her special signs because the shape of her hands was different from a chimpanzee's. Like Washoe, Koko learned signs for objects. But she could also make signs that stood for feelings like mad, sad and curious. Koko even invented some signs. She made up her own signs for "thermometer" and "stethoscope." Koko also named her pet kitten. She called it All Ball. Why such a strange name for a cat? The gray kitten had no tail and probably reminded Koko of a ball of fur.

In spite of all this signing, some scientists still think that chimpanzees and gorillas aren't really communicating. They think that the apes are just copying their trainers. What do you think?

All Ball

Koko

Index

Answers

Page 23
chimpanzee = I am angry
cheetah = I am listening
to something
hippopotamus = I am angry
dog = I am relaxed

Page 28
1. fiddler crab
2. mudskipper
3. wolf spider